THE RICHES
== OF ==
RESPECT

by

SAITIA FAAIFO

Bloomington, IN  Milton Keynes, UK

authorHOUSE™

AuthorHouse™
1663 Liberty Drive, Suite 200
Bloomington, IN 47403
www.authorhouse.com
Phone: 1-800-839-8640

AuthorHouse™ UK Ltd.
500 Avebury Boulevard
Central Milton Keynes, MK9 2BE
www.authorhouse.co.uk
Phone: 08001974150

First published by AuthorHouse 2/19/2007

ISBN: 1-4259-1260-5 (dj)
ISBN: 1-4259-1238-9 (sc)

Printed in the United States of America
Bloomington, Indiana

This book is printed on acid-free paper.

DEDICATION

I am dedicating this book to my beautiful, loving, mother, Eloise
Faaifo, and my strong, protective and humble father, Saitia Faaifo Sr.
Both of you have been my role models for hard work, dedication, and
unconditional love, that will influence my life forever!

ACKNOWLEDGMENTS

I WOULD LIKE TO ACKNOWLEDGE MY SIBLINGS: my brothers, Leonides "Tito" Echevarria, Michael Faaifo and my sisters, Vicky Echevarria, Ivette Echevarria and Vaiola Faaifo. Your collective strength, courage, faith and standing tall in times of difficulties, is a tribute to our family's love for life and for one another. I love you all. To my three beautiful children, Evangelique Faaifo, Saitia Faaifo and Amber Leilani Faaifo. Daddy loves you all with all his heart. To my close friend, Eric Karsaboom. Your 20 years of friendship has taught me a lot about integrity and character.

To my late publisher, Lakisha Marie Tanksley: Your belief in me has strengthened me. Your spirit lives on in me.

And to my partner in creating this book, Sally Schloss. Sally, thank you for your incredible gift in which our journey together went from "mind to manifestation" of this book. And thank you for your persistent passion in keeping me honest throughout. You are simply extraordinary! A true Angel.

I am also grateful to all the countless lives that have touched mine and helped shape me into the person I am today.

TABLE OF CONTENTS

Introduction:
The Riches of Respect

"There is a Vitality, a life force, an energy, a quickening, that is translated through you into action, and because there is only one of you, this expression is unique. And if you block it, it will never grow through any other medium, and will be lost."

–Martha Graham

"Whatever you do for yourself in life you take to your grave, but what you do for others you leave behind with them."

~LES BROWN

T HIS IS A BOOK ABOUT SURVIVING AND excelling, and the lessons that have enriched my life, and made my journey possible. I am sharing my story and knowledge in the hope of assisting others in their lives. This is not a book about how to get rich, (although material riches, even wealth can be a bi-product of these practices), but rather I'm speaking about the kind of riches that can enhance everyone's life: at work, at home, with strangers, bosses, friends, and loved ones. I'm speaking of the riches that come from leading a respectful life.

Respect is something earned, based on how you behave in the world. This comes from a deep place of compassion, love, and imaginatively knowing what it is like to walk in someone else's shoes. It is something that is sorely lacking in the world. In business, there are many managers who don't treat their employees with respect. People who are culturally different are often not respected, and some of today's youth disrespect their teachers, parents, and classmates.

The list of bad behavior is long: interrupting, harassing, bullying, punishing, victimizing, back talking, putting down, excluding, ignoring, making fun of, humiliating, and at it's worst, killing and warring.

What are the Results of Disrespect?

POOR STUDENT BEHAVIOR FORCES SCHOOLS TO become places where teachers have to discipline and maintain order rather than teach. Gang activity in both the inner city and suburbs has increased by 200% since 2002. Eighty-five percent of employees in America today feel unappreciated and unacknowledged for their contributions and hard work. Over half the families today don't have a father at home to help raise and protect their children. Racism is still destroying lives with hate crimes, or by limiting people's right to equal opportunities. Religious intolerance divides people and at its most destructive, leads to war and violence. Women worldwide are still suffering from the indignities and abuses of inequality.

I am not suggesting that the world is such a simple place that all problems are cured by the single practice of respect. However, I am saying that respect is such a fundamental and powerful behavior, that if embraced, will change your life, your relationships, and your world.

Why? Because every positive and satisfying human relationship is founded on mutual respect. Conversely, relationships deteriorate when there is a lack of respect. What marriage has a chance of surviving when one or both partners lose respect for each other? What child will listen to a parent if there is no respect? Without the role models of how to develop respectful human relations, how can we as a society, expect young people to not act out, and feel entitled to behave however they want?

In this book, I use myself and my experiences to tell a story that is, in the end, not about me. My story simply illustrates the principles and practices that I have adopted as a way of life, allowing me to rise from truly humble beginnings, to become a key manager at a major U.S. corporation, a leader, and a motivational speaker. My life is but one example of the riches that come to you when you lead a respectful life. I am hoping by reading this book that you will take away insights that you can, and will, apply in your own life. Because, after all, we all have the power to make the world a better place: one person at a time.

As you venture forth through these pages, please understand that every word that is written, every story told, is filled with love, honor, and respect for you, my dear reader.

NOTES:

NOTES:

NOTES:

Chapter One:
Who Am I?

"Make the most of yourself, for that is all there is of you"

–Ralph Waldo Emerson"

"If you want to build a very tall building, you have to dig a very deep foundation."

~ Brian Tracy

My name is Saitia Faaifo. I am first and foremost, a person. A person who is part Samoan and part Puerto Rican. I am also Hawaiian-born and raised. I am a U. S. citizen. I live and work stateside now, so I am also a San Franciscan, a west coaster, a northwest Californian.

My point about making all these distinctions is that there are many ways we classify people and use labels to provide short cuts to evaluate who they are. Some of these short cuts are useful because they provide a context and a way to relate. Some of these short cuts are damaging because they allow us to make assumptions that have little to do with who we are.

Some of who I am is accidental. It just so happened that my mother and father met and married and I was born. Some of who I am is inherited. I have my father's build, my mother's patience and calmness. What I *learned* from my parents has made a significant impact in my life. And my fathers Samoan ways or "Fa'a Samoa" has shown me the true meaning of respect for one another. The kind of person I've *chosen* to become is more important than what opportunities or lack of opportunities I started life with.

I was born on the island Oahu, Hawaii on October 3rd 1965 in a town called Kalihi. I was the first son of Saitia Faaifo Sr., and Eloise Faaifo. I have two brothers, Michael and Vaiola and three other siblings from my mother's first marriage: Vicky, Ttio and Ivette.

We all lived together as a very close-knit family and the first lesson that I learned early on was to respect my parents. Respecting my parents grew out of three things: the way they disciplined and loved me, by observing their work ethic, and how they were treated in the world.

I saw how hard my parents worked to keep us together, to provide for us. When I said that I came from humble beginnings, I meant we were poor. In the days of my early childhood there were times when all we had to eat for dinner was rice and ketchup. My siblings and I learned at a young age to help each other and to make sacrifices for the good of the group, for the family.

My Mother

MY MOTHER, ELOISE FAAIFO, WAS THE HARDEST working woman I've ever known. At one time she had over seven jobs, cleaning dental offices, medical suites and hotel rooms. She would get up at 4:00 A.M. to start her workday and would not come home until 10 P.M. at night.

I know when my mother came home because I came home with her. When I was ten years old, my mother picked me up after school so that I could help her finish off the second half of her day. Believe me there were other things that I wanted to do at that age, like be with my friends, or go the local arcade and play *Pacman* and *foosball*. But I also knew that I had to do my part, especially when I saw the terribly long hours my mother was working to help put food on our table.

What I couldn't have known when I started to help my mother was who she was in the world, or how she was perceived. Here was a woman with a third grade education, doing tiring, physical labor for twelve hours a day, yet she always carried herself with a great deal of self-respect. Everywhere we went we were warmly welcomed. At the medical offices and dental suites we cleaned, all the employees would greet us and tell me how wonderful my mother was. My mother was graceful and loving and everyone she worked for respected her.

It didn't matter what the job was or how tired she might be, it was her work ethic to do the best job possible. She showed respect to her employers as well as to herself. It was her performance, her integrity that was on the line. I began to understand that people will always engage with, and be appreciative of, someone that displays a positive and respectful attitude. It didn't matter that my mother had a humble position in the world. What did matter was that people adored her and that I was proud of her.

My Father

SAITIA FAAIFO SR., MY FATHER, STARTED AS A dishwasher and worked his way up to become Head Steward at the Kahala Hilton Hotel, one of the largest hotels on the island. The kitchen in which he began as a dishwasher, he now ran.

As a kid, my father took me to the Kahala Hilton for his annual overnight inventory. At this five star hotel, inventory is taken on every kitchen appliance, utensil, and piece of equipment in the kitchen department.

My dad would seat me in the famous hotel showroom that featured the legendary entertainer Danny Kelikini. I felt like royalty. Even though I was only about seven or eight years old, my father's co-workers, his boss, in fact all the employees were catering to me and my dad as though he was a king, and I was a prince. Even the great entertainer Danny Kelikini treated my dad like he was the owner of the hotel.

I remember one of my father's co-workers came up to me and said, "Hey little guy, are you Saitia's son?"

"Yes sir," I replied.

"You're dad is the best human being I've ever known. He is the most respected person in this entire company, even the President of the Hotel makes a point of coming to say hello to your dad. Whenever your dad needs something done at work, everyone does it quickly and efficiently."

My father was destined to rise in the ranks, not only through hard work but because he was one of those people who had a very charismatic presence. Good-looking, tall, well-built, he carried himself with a demeanor that made people notice him. I didn't matter if he was a dishwasher at one point in his life, or uneducated, or poor. He was a caring, warm, and energetic man who made people feel at ease and welcomed, and who commanded respect by treating other people well. Both my parents did. My parents weren't powerful people in the world in terms of money and status, but they were powerful in their influence and example.

Discipline and Love

WHEN I WAS ABOUT NINE YEARS OLD I MADE THE mistake of walking in-between the talking space of two adults. My father and my uncle were engaged in a conversation. As a response, my father hit me upside the head, looked at me and said severely, "Don't you ever walk between two adults talking unless you say in a very courteous way, 'excuse me.'"

When I was nine I really didn't understand why something so innocuous as interrupting would demand such a violent reaction. I didn't understand that this was how my father had been raised. The Samoan culture that he came from was very strict about what was appropriate and inappropriate behavior. As much as I may have resented it at the time, I can promise you that I never made that mistake again and to this day I consider it rude when someone barges into a conversation without expressing the common courtesy of saying excuse me.

Yet another lesson in respect, not quickly forgotten.

Responsibilities

IN MY FAMILY, CHORES WERE NOT OPTIONAL. IT wasn't something that our parents asked us to do because they thought it would teach us responsibility or help build character. Well, perhaps there was some of that in there. But as a family of eight, chores were done so that we could all survive together and not live in utter chaos and squalor. Since I did not have a TV mom who stayed at home all day, vacuuming in her shirtwaist dress and high heels, I worked, we all worked, and we all started young.

When I was around seven years old, before I was old enough to help my mother at her jobs, I was assigned yard duties, along with my brother, Michael. As soon as Michael and I got home from school we had to clean our front and back yard: Michael in the front and me in the back. The reason we had to maintain our yards every day was because of the abundance of leaves that would fall from our banana, taro, and plumeria trees. We also mowed the lawn, cut hedges, raked the grass.

We rushed to our duties the second we walked in the house, because these jobs had to be done before my father came home. My father's discipline was swift and uncompromising, and neither my brother nor I wanted to be on the receiving end of it.

Before you get the wrong impression and think that my dad was all discipline, (as you can see, he was very strict by today's standards), you should also know that he worshipped the ground I walked on, and made me feel very loved. Part of showing that love, (I came to understand in maturity), was holding me to a high standard to prepare me for being in the world.

A different expression of how my father demonstrated that he cared about me was when he gave me a dollar to get to school, knowing that I only needed a quarter. Or when my parents fought, (which all parents do on occasion), it was my dad who splurged on ice cream, a luxury item for us, in order to put smiles back on our anxious faces. My dad knew that taking us for ice cream was a gesture that showed us that he cared about our happiness, and that everything would be all right.

Pivotal Moments in My Youth

Mrs. Lee

SEVERAL TIMES A MONTH, MY MOTHER TOOK ME with her to help clean a huge mansion in the beautiful Honolulu hills. Mrs. Lee, the owner of this luxurious home, was in her early sixties. As I emptied the garbage cans and ashtrays I would marvel at how huge this house was; three stories tall. The best part of this house for me was the many bowls of candy lying about. Mrs. Lee made it my responsibility to taste the candy to see if it was fresh or stale. As you might imagine, that was a really tough job for a ten year old.

One day, after having thought about this a lot, I decided to ask Mrs. Lee a question. Her answer has influenced me my whole life. Her answer is something I have never forgotten.

"Mrs. Lee, how did you get so wealthy and get to have such a big home?" It was a brazen question to ask, but I just couldn't contain myself. I had to know.

Mrs. Lee leaned over a bit, bending down towards me as she looked me square in the eye, and said, "Young man, whatever you do in life, whether you're a garbage man, a lawyer, or a doctor, you be the very best there is!

Mrs. Lee was a realtor and apparently she had been the very best. Her answer resonated inside me like a secret for success.

Basketball

IN HIGH SCHOOL I WAS VERY ATHLETIC. I PLAYED
basketball and football. However, in my sophomore and junior years
I had to stop because I had to help my mother after school. In my
senior year I begged my mother and father to let me play basketball
again. It was my last year after all. I knew I was good and that I
could contribute to the team. Finally, I convinced my parents to
have my brother substitute for me with my mom.

My coach had a sharp tongue and would really belittle people.
Throughout my Junior year, whenever my coach saw me he would
harass me. I had explained my reason for not playing for two years,
that I couldn't go to practice after school, that I was helping my
mother, my family, but it didn't seem to make an impression on him.
He still rode me every chance he got.

When sign up day came in my Senior year, my coach saw me in
line and started saying in a very loud voice, in front of all the other
students, "leave the auditorium, Faaifo, because you're not going to
play for me. You'll never make the team. Why are you signing up?
You're wasting your time."

Guys were laughing at me, but I kept moving through the line
until I got to the sign up sheet. "You're wasting your time," the
coach repeated, but it was my last year and by god I was going to
play basketball. I looked at him and said I was going to sign this
paper anyway. The assistant coach laughed, "He's wasting his time."
Everybody was making fun of me. I signed the register and then I
turned and walked away.

One hundred people came to the tryouts. I made the first cut.
Then I made the second cut and the third and then I was on the

team. I became one of the top scorers. I made the newspapers. When the team was in a crisis, the coach put me in. He developed this bond with me and by the end of the basketball season everybody was calling me, "the coach's son."

As Frank Sinatra once said, "the greatest revenge in life is massive success."

In 1983, my high school basketball team went to Japan for a tournament. It was an experience of a lifetime. If I had walked away and given up basketball, I never would have learned that perseverance leads to unanticipated opportunities. It taught me to trust myself. Whenever I make up my mind to do something, I do it. I had choices at that moment of sign up. I could have quit trying. I could have angrily told the coach to shut up. But I wasn't disrespectful. I walked away. I let my actions do my talking.

"Do it, even when others don't believe in you."

~LES BROWN

LEADING BY EXAMPLE

A Lesson in Leadership From My Father

I THINK MOST SONS WANT TO BE LIKE THEIR fathers. I always wanted the same respect that my father commanded. I thought he was an incredible man.

I remember one incident that exemplified my father's behavior, and showed me how to be a man. This had a powerful influence on me when I had to deal with a bullying manager years later in one of my first jobs.

When I was around ten years old, there was a bully in my neighborhood who was about fifteen years old. One day, he hit my younger brother, who was only eight. The bully was much bigger than my brother, at least twice his size. My brother came home very hurt and cried to my mom. He didn't know what to do. My dad found out and went over to the house where the bully lived and found the dad sitting on the porch. My father said, "You let your son beat up my son. You're a man and I'm a man. Now you stand up and we'll settle this like men." The guy refused to stand up. I don't blame him. My dad was a hell of a big guy. The outcome was that the bully stopped picking on my brother.

I respected my father for that. It may not be my way, today, but the meaning of the event was that you need to confront that which is threatening to you and yours. You stand up. I have no idea what my father's fears were or are. I do know that in the community, at work, at home, he demonstrated to me several ways of showing respect and commanding the respect of others that has been a role model for me in my life. The lesson? You don't let people disrespect you. You earn respect by refusing to tolerate abuse. It needn't be a challenge to fight. There are many ways to earn respect. I have my own version of what my father did which will be described in the next chapter.

A Lesson In Leadership From My Heart

THERE IS ONE OTHER STORY THAT I WANT TO share that represents leading by example. It comes from my own adolescent experience. It was a decision I made that wasn't consciously informed by my wanting to be a leader. It was born out of a place of compassion for a student that was being ridiculed.

A young woman in my school had a disfigured face. For this, she was taunted and treated cruelly by other students. She had suffered her whole life from being laughed at and called names. One day, in the lunchroom, this poor girl who was sitting alone, trying to be invisible and just eat her lunch was unable to escape being made an object of fun. I couldn't stand it anymore. I was lucky in that my looks helped make me popular. My good looks and her unfortunate looks had nothing to do with either of us. It was an accident of birth. I was no more responsible for my face than she was for hers. What I could be responsible for, however, was how I behaved. I knew that my popularity would command a different reaction from onlookers than anything she could possibly do to help herself.

I stood up from my table of friends, walked across the lunchroom and sat down across from her with my lunch tray. I'm sure she thought, now what? Here comes another joke at my expense. I looked at her and said quietly, "It's okay. Just look at me."

It took me a little while to coax her to look up and when she did she gave me the tiniest of smiles. I stayed with her throughout lunch and the taunting and jeering stopped. People I'm sure were shocked, but I was determined to protect her with my status and immunity from being picked on. For the rest of the school term no more cruel jokes were made. I only wish that protection from such insensitivity could have followed her everywhere in her life. I knew, had learned, what other kids apparently had not by that age. That she was a human being just like me and was entitled to being treated respectfully and with dignity.

These are my roots, my foundation. These stories have helped shape me.

NOTES:

NOTES:

NOTES:

CHAPTER TWO:
RESPECT IN THE WORKPLACE

"Life shrinks or expands in proportion to ones courage"

–ANAIS NIN

"A candle loses nothing, when it lights another candle."

~THOMAS JEFFERSON

IN JANUARY OF 1987, I MOVED FROM HONOLULU, Hawaii to Northern California. I was nineteen years old. My first job there was at a manufacturing company in Hayward, California. I was what you would call a journeyman. My job function was to transfer the cow meat and shank (calf) to and from the refrigerators. Our supervisor was mean and cutting. He would quickly jump on an employee for the most trivial things. He would yell at us and treat us like we weren't human, like we were as unfeeling and uncomprehending as the meat we were handling. He never showed us any respect. I already knew that one day it would be my turn to be yelled at.

One morning as I was doing my best to keep a low profile and just do my job, it happened. After he yelled at me, he quickly walked away as if rushing to get into his office. In the heat of the moment I walked after him and before he could shut his office door, I caught up to him, looked him in the eye, and to his amazement I said, "Who do you think you are? I don't need you or this job. If you don't respect me or my work then the hell with you." Then I walked off and went right back to my workstation and finished out the day.

The next morning when I came back to work instead of firing me, he promoted me. He called a meeting and informed our team that starting today, Saitia Faaifo would be his foreman.

Wow. I had faced down my own bully and I realized right then and there, that I had been promoted because I demanded that I be respected. I also learned as Ralph Waldo Emerson wrote, "If you face your fears, then the death of fear is certain."

I love the story that Les Brown tells of a little boy walking home from school. Every day, on a particular block, a bulldog would chase him and every day he would run terrified. One day, the little boy got tired of running and being scared and decided that the next time he encountered the dog he would throw something at it.

The next day, right on schedule the bulldog appeared. The boy picked up a brick and as he cocked his arm to throw, he looked at the dog and realized the dog didn't have any teeth.

Most of us are running from things that have no teeth. My supervisor had a loud bark, but when I stood up to him, he too had no teeth. Whatever you're running from, stop and face it head on. You will overcome.

Building Success From Within Oneself

WHY IS IT THAT MOST PEOPLE WALK AWAY FROM their dreams before they even start their adult life? Les Brown, once said, "Most people's dreams have been beaten out of them through this experience called life." Many people in fact are dream busters. "You can't do that." "That's impossible." "It'll never happen." "Are you crazy?" If I had listened to the negative advice of friends and enemies throughout my life, I would never have been able to make a positive impact on my own life and the lives of the people I've had the honor of coming in contact with. If I had listened to those people, I wouldn't have had the life that has led me to write this book.

So, how did a poor kid from Hawaii, with only a high school education, manage to go from a warehouse worker to operations manager at Comcast, one of the largest and most successful corporations in the world today? How did this same kid manage to get eighteen promotions in twenty years of work?

The answer is through practicing respect, taking initiative, being a continuous learner and being a leader.

Earning Respect

IN 1995, WHEN I WAS 24 YEARS OLD, I WORKED AS A supervisor for a huge grocery food distributor. I had a crew of about

35 employees. Because of the multi-ethnic communities in and around the San Francisco Bay area, we were facing new challenges in the area of diversity and communications. The problem was so overwhelming that our company president decided to call a meeting.

Our president went around the room and asked each of the supervisors and managers to provide feedback on what was going on in their department, so as to shed some light on the communications problems. The first manager said, "Well this is America, not the Philippines, and if they don't speak English, that's just too bad." The second manager added, "Yeah, this isn't Mexico. In America, we speak English. If they don't, that's not my problem." Then I stood up and said, "Well, I don't speak Filipino or Spanish, but I do speak RESPECT. And if you don't speak that language then your employees will know it and they will definitely not give you their best."

What really astounds me about the attitude expressed in that room is that everyone there had descended from immigrants: just from different groups, at different periods of time. America was built by immigrants. Our diversity and the contributions of so many different cultures, points-of-view, and capabilities is what makes us great. Each new wave of immigrants revitalizes our culture and provides the backbone of our economy. Who else but the new immigrant populations, who have nothing, would be willing to work hard for low wages in jobs other Americans would prefer not to do? They are the ones that have the dream to improve their lives and to make it here with a fervor and ambition unknown to people whose lives are easier. Diversity isn't the issue. Prejudice and lack of patience and understanding of people who are "different," "new," "foreign," "not us," is the issue. The only way to break down that barrier and develop understanding and tolerance is through respect.

You see, I truly believe that respect is the one language that everyone immediately understands. People know when they are on the receiving end of contempt. They also know when they are being treated respectfully and with kindness. It is simply a universal language and anyone can speak it. When spoken, it produces wonderful results. People begin to trust and open up. Most importantly, people move from being perceived as "other" to becoming, "one of us." The dynamics of the relationship change and people become supportive: and that works both ways.

Being Respectful

"People don't care how much you know, until they know how much you care about them."

~ Zig Ziglar

WHEREVER I WORK, EVERYBODY KNOWS ME. There's a reason for that. One of the things I do as a leader is make sure that my employees, especially the women, feel respected and appreciated. I always try to understand their dreams and what is important to them in their lives. For instance, I used to work in Palo Alto before I got promoted to San Francisco, and there was a woman named Tamara who worked there for me. She had two sons, Daniel and Cy. Cy played baseball on Sundays, so on Monday mornings when I came to work, I would always ask, how was Cy's baseball game? Did his team win? The fact that I truly am interested gets communicated because you can't fake this stuff. It has to be real and come from your heart.

Later, when I was in a pinch and had to go to Tamara and say, "Listen Tamara, I need some performance reports quickly, can I count on you?" She always would say, "Of course you can count on me, Sai." So it's reciprocal. She is motivated to help me because she knows that I am sincerely interested in her as a human being. I don't remember her kid's names just so that she will work harder for me. I know how good it feels to be seen and heard and respected. I also know what it's like to be on the receiving end of being treated like you're invisible.

Another example is Blytha, the dispatch manager, who works in the same San Francisco office I work in. She has a daughter named Jamaica. One Friday, when we were talking in a meeting, I asked her how Jamaica was doing in college, and she seemed surprised that I would remember and that I would ask.

These behaviors take only a few minutes but the relationship it builds and the way you make a person feel, can last forever. I believe in making peace, not waging war with my employees. Being a critical, micromanaging boss only causes resentment, and you wind up with passive-aggressive employees who are part of the problem, instead of being part of the solution. When I need to get the best of my employees, when I need to get us all, as a team, to give 100% to get a job done, my team will reach down deep inside themselves, because they want me, and all of us to be successful. It's all about people. It doesn't matter what industry I'm in. I am in the people business. I wish everyone understood that as a leader.

I took all the girls in our dispatch department out to lunch. They work directly with my field team. They don't report to me, but I told them, because you work with me indirectly, I'm going to thank you all by taking you to lunch. I had a chance to talk to them about their lives, their dreams, how their children are doing and they told me, "Sai, we have never had any manager take us out like this. Never."

I said, "I can't control that but I can control this, right here, right now." That's another lesson. I can't control other people's behavior. In fact I can't "control" anything. But I can do what I believe in, what I think is right and try to make a difference.

Every time I see those women, they always welcome me warmly. "Sai, how're you doing?" "Good morning, Sai." There is only one reason for this. I got to know them as people. It's easy. So many times people treat you like a number or with disrespect. It's been shown time and again that the most important thing to people on a job is not the pay. After receiving a raise, even a large raise, if people are unhappy at their job, the lift they get from the raise lasts maybe three weeks. Then they go back to being miserable. The most important thing for people is being treated well, being recognized, and being able to do their best, using the skills and talents they have. That is experienced as a greater reward than money.

"If you see a turtle on the fence, that turtle didn't get there by itself."

The author, John C. Maxwell wrote that in one of his wonderful books. It's a true statement, and very powerful. Nobody gets there by them selves. It's people that help you get to where you want to be.

Poor managers don't understand that. Managers, who make their employees the enemy, or try to control them to make them productive, are creating misery and lack of cooperation in the workplace. Passion, support, consideration, recognition, and respect are what will put a manager on the top. A truly great manager helps *others* become "turtles on the fence."

Continuous Learner

I REMEMBER MY FIRST LEADERSHIP TEAM meeting. I gave everyone on my team a leadership book to read. They looked at me somewhat confused, so I said to them, "Perhaps not all readers are leaders, but all leaders are readers." This was a quote from Brian Tracy, and I have always taken it to heart.

Other managers found out that I gave books to my team and they pretty much thought it was ridiculous. They weren't quite so smug when my team won three sales campaigns in a row. One manager in particular who was especially critical of my management style, wound up eating crow, since his team finished in last place in the sales competitions.

Over the course of my twenty years in the work world, I have experienced resistance to change and have been dismissed and ridiculed for efforts I have made to bring about change. When I was a manger in my twenties I was often condescended to by peers who were much more senior in years. Who is this twenty-something Island boy who presumes to tell us he knows better?

If it weren't for my successes I would have been discouraged long ago. Part of what has sustained me and driven me to ignore these nay sayers is the mentoring I have gotten from books. I realized at an early age in my career that if I wanted to succeed, I needed knowledge. If I wanted to create change and follow my passion for making a difference in the workplace and in the community I had to learn how to put my beliefs into action. I immersed myself in every business book I could get my hands on and committed to memory quotes and passages that impressed me. Just because I didn't get support on the job, didn't mean that I couldn't find answers from people who had been very successful. I have found that success is often accompanied by respect for others and a sense of generosity, of giving back. At least those are the people I choose to listen to and learn from. My models, Les Brown, Brian Tracy, John C. Maxwell, and Zig Ziglar, to name a few, have been writers who have helped me to develop tools and ideas that have sustained me and improved my performance as an employee and a leader.

And that is why I hand out books at my team meetings. I implement the strategies that have worked for me. If I can inspire my team, individual, by individual, to embrace personal growth and to develop a common language for succeeding, then I am empowering them to do their best for themselves, as well as for the group as a whole. They know that I care about them and that is why they respect and embrace the things I do to cheer them on. The reward is to win. We all want to be part of a winning team. As their coach, it is my job to help them get there.

Being Inventive and Having Fun

I MADE A VIP PIN FOR EVERY MEMBER ON MY TEAM, because to me they are the most important people I serve, and they know it. So, instead of thinking it was a silly gesture, they proudly wore their pins.

When you walk by our team meeting room, you hear laughter and enthusiasm. I begin or end meetings with quotes and discussions about the meaning of the quote. They affectionately tease me about it, but they would be disappointed if I didn't include it. In fact they speak up and ask, "What's the quote this week Sai?"

"Why is there so much laughing going on at Sai's meetings," I've heard asked. "How can Sai's team be so productive when all I hear is laughter coming from the room." If only they would understand that having fun is one of the secrets to our success.

Sharing Information

SOMETHING I BELIEVE IN DOING ON A WEEKLY basis is sharing the reality of where we are in relation to our goals. We celebrate our successes and we roll up our sleeves to be more productive and bring our numbers up when our performance is lagging behind. By sharing this information I keep things above board and keep people motivated.

The old cliché, "knowledge is power" is a cliché for a reason. It's true. People who withhold knowledge are trying to maintain a power position for themselves. People create a different culture when they are confident that their power is not lost by being open and generous, The culture that I am invested in is an egalitarian one in which there are no secrets; and therefore there is no opportunity for paranoia and pitting people against each other as they jockey for status.

Leaders are motivators, coaches and mentors, and overseers of performance. They are responsible for the good of the whole and they are the reality check for how the group is doing. At least that's how it should be. At least that's how I see it and try to do it.

Taking Initiative

FIFTEEN YEARS AGO WHEN I WAS 23, I HAD A brilliant manager named David Klecker. He taught me how to organize a spreadsheet and do the numbers so as to create transparency in tracking the success of a process or system, or to identify "what was wrong with this picture." It is a model that I have used in every job I've had and that I use to this day with my team. Once a month we look at the spreadsheet as a group to see how many hours have been worked, how many sales made, how many points earned, how many benchmarks have been met, etc. It allows us to evaluate our progress as we go, and to make performance adjustments. This openness also allows for input and sharing of ideas as to how we can improve.

The first time I effectively used this system was when I was 24 years old and was promoted to warehouse superintendent, overseeing 110 employees and 18 million dollars worth of product. When I assumed this position, the company had lots of people in the warehouse working overtime and we were eating up a lot of money in overtime pay. We had two supervisors: one for the morning shift, 4:00 a.m. to 12:30 p.m. and one for the day shift, 5:00 pm to 1:30 am. With the shift gap, each shift would often end up working overtime putting in a twelve to fifteen hour day. It was crazy and completely out of control. People were burning out and quitting. Replacing and training people meant more money lost to the company. I did my spreadsheet and ran the numbers. I had an idea. I called the president of the company and asked him if he would be interested in saving the company $120,000 a year.

I told him I wanted to bring on one more supervisor for a 10:00 a.m. to 6:30 p.m. middle shift, with fifteen employees working straight time only. We had languishing Fresno accounts and I wanted that shift to pick up those accounts. Basically, by opening up another shift I eliminated any need for overtime and Fresno got the attention it needed. This improvement reduced overtime hours from 65 a week to almost zero. We reduced our turnover ratio from 75% to a more normal 10% and hugely improved employee morale. We also increased our productivity and considerably improved our service performance. And, finally, as projected, it saved the company $120,000.

Being a Leader

IN MY COMPANY, I HAVE BEEN GIVEN THE opportunity to speak to other managers about what it takes to be a leader. This is my vision: to transform management behavior and understanding, so that employees will come to work each day motivated to do a great job because they are happy to be there. Companies win, managers win and most of all, employees win.

I am going to share some of the content from my manager leadership presentation—the part that isn't company specific, and that would be relevant to any manager. I hope there are quotes, attitudes, and ideas that you can take away from this and use yourself. It doesn't matter if you aren't a manager at present. Perhaps the information will help inspire you to become a leader in your company.

Motivational Concepts

THERE IS A BIBLE QUOTE THAT SAYS, "WHERE there is no vision, people perish." But I say, "When you give them a vision, people flourish."

Vision is the key to human accomplishment. Without it, without leaders of vision, people get lost, get stuck and can even "perish." With vision, people have purpose, can focus, and commit. They know where they're going and why they are going there.

A survey was conducted with over 20,000 employees from four different companies asking what they needed and wanted the most from their work experience. Number one was appreciation for what they did for the company. Number two, was understanding the vision of where the company was going in the future, and who was going to take them there. Surprisingly, third on the list was money.

What this tells us is that we, as leaders, are responsible for sharing the vision the company has for itself and its employees going forward into the future. But we must also have a vision for everyday, that lets each person know how they fit into the larger plan, and how their contributions matter. Making people feel important and connected to the big picture, making them understand how they serve the vision of the future, and that they are the vehicle for getting the company there, lets people know that they are significant and appreciated. Too many times people feel that what they do has no impact. They can't see beyond their own cubbyhole or their tasks. Managers will say, "You don't need to know that. Just do your job," failing to recognize that the person asking does need to know—or they wouldn't be asking. For instance, it may help them understand how their job supports someone else in a totally different part of the company. Or, being given the context for what they do prevents them from making mistakes out of ignorance. My point being, that vision in all its manifestations, allows people to "flourish."

Let me give you one example of a real world situation that I experienced. This was when I was a young man and was fairly new to being a manager. However, I had three things going for me: I had a commitment to be the best manager I could be, (good old Mrs. Lee's influence), I had Dave Klecker's, performance accountability system that he had taught me, and I had an attitude of respect toward my employees.

I was in charge of the night crew. I implemented my "Performance Snapshot," which for the first time since people had worked there, gave them actual feedback on their daily production numbers. My employees could see the impact their performance had on the company on a day-to-day basis. I challenged my team to be the best they could be. In fact, because I respected them, shared my vision with them, and assisted them in meeting, and exceeding the company's daily goals, we all rose to a new level together.

The improvement in the night crew's performance got my operations manager's attention and he promoted me to the dayshift to improve performance there as well. I was also promoted to ease the tensions between the employees and management. My behavior as a result of my attitude was as much responsible for the promotion, as my ability to measure success and tangibly show results. The outcome was that I reduced overtime and improved overall performance within two months.

Why am I on the Payroll?

USUALLY WHEN I ASK THAT QUESTION EVERYBODY gets quiet. Then I tell them why I'm on the payroll: because I want to make a difference at Comcast, and I signed up to be a leader. Then I tell a story…

At the turn of the twentieth century a leading industry in the United States was the railroad industry. Mr. Winston was the President of one of the powerful railroad lines. One day, Mr. Winston decided to take a ride. He got off at one of the railroad stations where he saw two of his employees on the platform. One employee was someone he knew. His name was Marvin. When Marvin saw Mr. Winston getting off the train, he went up to him and said, "Hi, Mr. Winston. How are you doing?" Mr. Winston said, "Well, hello Marvin. I'm fine. How are you?" Marvin asked after Mr. Winston's wife, Mary, and Mr. Winston asked after Marvin's wife, Lisa. The other employee watched in amazement as Mr. Winston and Marvin hugged and then parted.

When Marvin returned and sat down on the bench, the other employee, unable to contain his himself, immediately asked, "Marvin, how do you know the president of the company? Marvin replied, "Oh Mr. Winston and I were hired by the company on the same day thirty years ago."

The other employee said to Marvin, "I don't mean to embarrass you but why is he the president and why are you still sitting here?"

Marvin said, "You know, I've lost a lot of sleep over that through the years. Thirty years ago I came here to work for a $1.30 an hour. Thirty years ago, Mr. Winston came here to work for the railroad."

In other words, Mr. Winston came to devote all his efforts to the business, and Marvin came to collect a check.

One of the eye opening experiences I had was when I was a manager for a grocery distributor. It was a union shop, and it was the first time that I experienced a worker mentality dedicated to slowing down production in order to force the company to hire more people, which in turn would generate more union dues to satisfy the corrupt union organizers. The sad thing is that unions were originally formed to protect worker's rights. Today, in many instances, it's all about money, and unions have the reputation of sabotaging business. I got to see an example, first hand of people motivated by the paycheck and abandoning values that would allow the company and the workers to win.

I was determined to not have my team operate out of this thinking. Other managers were there because of seniority, years of service, rather than high performance. My challenge to myself was to earn the right to be, and remain a manager, based on performance alone. There was a huge gulf in this company between employees and management over the perceived and often real differences between these groups. I spent time getting to know my people as individuals. I was consistent, fair, and firm in my expectations of them. I built my team's morale and they performed. I earned my team's respect, because I respected them. I was the only manager in the three years that I worked there that never received one single grievance from an employee. (A grievance is a complaint that union employees can file against management whenever they feel like they've been treated unfairly).

What I really accomplished at this company was modeling a work ethic and style of leadership that wasn't about collecting a paycheck. Respect was established and my team wasn't motivated to participate in corrupt practices. They stopped merely collecting a paycheck too.

A company's greatest asset are its employees.

WHEN I SPEAK TO OTHER MANAGERS, I MAKE THE statement, "If this building burned down today and we collectively went across the street to another building, in about five or six hours we could run another operation with the brain power and knowledge our employees possess."

A company is its people. Treating people well should be the number one priority of any organization. The pain that so many people are in because of on the job stress is an unfortunate and common phenomenon. When we realize how the collection of human beings that fill a business and make it run are the brain trust of that company, that they are the ones that make the sales, build the products, provide the services, assist customers, and devote forty or more hours a week to making all this and more happen, how can you not be impressed with the people who serve this enterprise?

When you step back and take a look at the big picture, focusing on the collective group of employees rather than on individuals, you will see that they are the unsung heroes, the backbone of the company, and the world. Managers can do their part by supporting their people, by being excellent managers rather than incompetent, de-motivating, unappreciative managers. That isn't to say there aren't poor workers and people whose work ethic is non-existent and whose performance makes them undeserving of being employed. But most people really want to do well and want to be useful and want leaders who will help them perform at their best.

Giving an employee praise for doing a good job, giving an employee recognition for excellence so that peers and management know how well they've done, is often more motivating than any pay raise. That's one of the reasons I give out VIP pins to my team, because to me they are Very Important People, and I want them to know I value them, and I want others to have visual evidence of that appreciation.

The Director From Hell

LET ME GIVE YOU ONE EXAMPLE FROM MY LIFE OF how challenging being an advocate for change in an organization can be. I will call this story, The Director From Hell.

In the 1990s, I interviewed for a management position with the Director of Operations. When I met him, he was very cold and throughout the interview he never made eye contact with me. He made me feel very uneasy in his presence and it was clear to me that this person had no people skills.

Despite my unnerving interview, I was hired and took the job as receiving supervisor. Shortly after I started there, the director challenged my decision-making abilities. He especially got upset when I displayed my "Respect 1st attitude," with my employees. His style of management was that of intimidation. He was from the east coast with a hard-ass, New York manner. After months of harassment from this man, I got wind of the fact that he was bad mouthing me to others. I'd had it, so I went to our Human Resources Department (HR) to report what was going on. Fortunately, HR was already well aware of the director's poor attitude and management skills. I was not the first to complain. HR called our corporate office in Florida and they ran a formal investigation, which resulted in the director receiving a stern warning about his behavior.

Three months later, the director, again tried to "write me up," for not performing my job well. This time I challenged him in his office, telling him that I knew he was upset with me for standing up to him and I knew that he was trying to find excuses to terminate me.

Again HR got involved. This time a vice president from our corporate office flew in to investigate. The outcome was that the director was fired for harassment.

The source of all this trouble between us was that I sought to empower my people and the director competed with and belittled his. The director only respected managers who used his same methods of disrespect and intimidation. Because I refused to adopt those methods, and did not allow myself to be intimidated by him, he despised and persecuted me. Clearly, the real root of his behavior was that I threatened him. Being successful with my methods was a direct rebuke, a slap in his face. The consequences of his behavior and mine, the different choices we made given the situation, resulted in his being eliminated and all his employees getting relief from his toxic management style. Their morale was boosted and their performance improved.

I was lucky. My company researched the situation and supported me. In another company, where such resources aren't in place, or where the authority figure has a great deal of power, I might have been the one fired. That is why I believe that educating managers on how to encourage, enable motivate, and respect their people is of paramount importance in every company. That message is one of the reasons I am writing this book.

My Creed

I do not choose to be a common man.
It is my right to be uncommon...if I can.
I seek opportunity...not security.
I do not wish to be a kept citizen, humbled
and dulled by having the state look after me.
I want to take a calculated risk;
to dream and to build, to fail and to succeed.
I refuse to barter incentive for a dole.
I prefer the challenges of life to the guaranteed
existence to the stale calm of Utopia.
I will not trade freedom for beneficence
nor my dignity for a handout.
I will never cower before any master
nor bend to any threat.

It is my heritage to stand erect, proud
and unafraid; to think and act for myself;
enjoy the benefits of my creations
and to face the world boldly
and say, this I have done.
All this is what it means to be an
American.

By DEAN ALFANGE

STRENGTH IN UNITY

ONE CLYDESDALE PONY CAN PULL 1,500 POUNDS, but two Clydesdale ponies can pull over 5,000 pounds. There is strength in unity.

We are unstoppable when we all work together. I have a wonderful group of leaders that report to me. I always make it a point to identify and acknowledge their team's strengths in our monthly group meetings, because they are responsible for those successes. One of my leader's teams has outstanding sales figures, another team has incredibly consistency numbers, another team is resilient and hungry to learn more, and yet another group produces high productivity numbers. By deliberately making an effort to highlight all their strengths in front of their peers I am empowering them and giving them the recognition they deserve for their contributions to our company. Because, I always remind them, "Together we win!"

Respect For Diversity and Differences In A Multi-Cultural Society

"TAKE ME FOR INSTANCE," I TELL OTHER MANAGERS, "I was born in rural Hawaii, my family was poor, and here I am today in San Francisco running a quarter of a billion dollar business, as part of the management team. If I can do it, then anybody can do it. You never know who the next rising star in your organization will be. The most unlikely people can succeed in this world. Your assumptions about what a person's capabilities are, superficially based on the package they come in, or their education, or status, places limitations on people where none belong. Stereotyping people and prejudice are the biggest barriers to success in a multi-cultural society—not the people themselves."

"We Will Not Go Where The Path Is. We Will Pave Our Own Path and Leave A Trail."

~ UNKNOWN

We have to be uncommon. We have to make a difference. As leaders, it is our obligation to "leave a trail," for others to follow.

On my team for example I lead by motivating and inspiring, by recognizing and rewarding, and by sharing knowledge. From V.I.P. pins for my team to the books I give them to read, to lunches we share getting to know one another, to strategy sessions and motivational speeches: all of it contributes to a management model that has proven to be successful and that anyone can adopt.

I want every member on my team to be strong. I encourage each of them to be uncommon, to think for themselves, to ask questions, to not be shy about seeking answers until there is understanding. I don't make people feel stupid for not knowing or not "getting it" immediately. I build their confidence rather than tear it down. Many managers, who are inappropriately critical, sabotage performance by undermining their employees. I'm not saying that mistakes, poor performance, bad attitude shouldn't be dealt with firmly. I am saying that the way in which you handle it makes all the difference.

When I was a young and callow manager of a warehouse, I was confronted by a situation with an employee that I would handle differently today. This story serves to show how inexperience and stress works against a desirable outcome. However, the story also demonstrates how the president of the company encouraged and supported me as a manager, building my confidence.

I needed a leader to assist my night crew, so I hired a supervisor named Mike. Every day I would meet with Mike for a few minutes then leave a laundry list of duties that I needed completed by the following day. After about two months on the job, I noticed that Mike's attitude towards me had changed. He became negative about everything and he started to show disrespect towards me. The huge responsibility that I had been given as the manager of this entire facility made me very impatient with poor attitudes. One day before his shift, Mike came in and as I gave him my list of assigned duties to complete, he said, "I don't like the way you operate this place."

I said, "Excuse me?"

He then repeated, "I don't like the way you run this place."

So I said, "Mike, if you don't like the way I run my operation, then I suggest you go work somewhere else."

"What did you say?" Mike said. So I repeated it. Mike barged out of my office and went straight to the president of our company in the building across the street. About thirty minutes later the president called me on the phone and said, "One of your supervisors was here. Mike said that you told him, if he didn't like the way you run your business, he should go work somewhere else."

I replied, "Well yes sir, that is what I said."

"Well then Sai, looks like your taking care of business. Thank you," and he hung up.

What I failed to do as a manger was take the time to find out what the problem was. How was I myself behaving as a manager that turned this employee off so badly after two months? Was it really even about me? Without discussing it, I couldn't know. I lost someone who may have been a perfectly good employee if I had had the experience, wisdom and insight to handle things differently. I didn't make the effort to respect where he was coming from. Instead, I took it personally. I also let things slide until there was enough resentment on his part that things blew up. Now it's also possible that no matter what I had done, this person would have behaved in exactly the same way, but I'll never know. I do know that I didn't give him the chance to change and behave differently.

The most impressive part of this story to me is that the president of the company supported my decision, sending me the message that he believed in me. That boosted my confidence tremendously. He had allowed me to exercise my own judgment, and didn't second-guess me, which would have undermined my authority. He trusted me. That was huge for me.

"It's not your aptitude but your attitude that determines your altitude."

~ BRIAN TRACY

I tell my people, I don't care about your technical mastery, or how qualified you are, if you don't have a great attitude that comes along with your aptitude, then I really can't use you.

Charles Swindell once said, *"The longer I live in life, the more I realize the impact attitude has on my life."*

Attitude is more important than facts. Attitude is more important than education and money and circumstances, and failures and successes and what other people think, or say or do. Attitude is more important than giftedness and skill and appearances. Attitude can make or break a home. Attitude can make or break a company and it can make or break you.

The remarkable thing about attitude is that everyday when we get up, we have a choice. We can choose the attitude we want to embrace for that day. We cannot control the inevitable. We cannot control the past. The one thing we can control is our attitude. I'm convinced that attitude is ten percent of what happens to me and ninety percent, of how I react to it.

Throughout my career I have been faced with unforeseen challenges. However I have always been able to bring my positive attitude to the forefront of any given situation.

For example, this morning in my managers meeting, my colleagues and I were asked by our director to revise the current work schedule within our departments in an effort to improve our customer relations. While other managers started objecting and looking for reasons why they couldn't do it, I picked up my phone, called my leadership team, explained the value and importance of adjusting our work schedule and within a few short minutes, got the buy-in and commitment from my team and smoothly made the critical operational transition. While others were finding ways out of it, I already had my entire staff ONBOARD.

Seven Letters to Live By

Responsibility

The best ability is to have response-ability. We as leaders signed up to be responsible for our team. We need to make an effort to do the right thing as leaders for our company.

Enthusiasm

You have to get excited about what you do for your company. Winston Churchill once said, *"Courage is going from failure to failure without losing enthusiasm."*
We need to make sure that even though we fail, we pick each other up and keep going moving forward.

Sense of Purpose

Our sense of purpose, our mission is to provide value to our customers day in and day out. Everybody has a purpose. Life has a purpose. Know and stay focused on the purpose of your business.

Positive Attitude

There are many attitudes you can bring with you to work each day. Oh, it's Monday and I'd rather stay in bed. Or, I wish I could call in sick. But getting up and starting the day as a gift that is being offered to you, whatever that day brings, is to live in the moment, with the expectation of things going great for you. The proverbial glass is half full point-of-view, instead of the glass is half-empty. Problems are opportunities for growth and understanding. See them as challenges that whet your appetite, inspiring you to find a better way that allows you to use your brain creatively.

Excellence

Make sure we do *all* we can do. And always do it right. If we get it right the second time, it means we should have gotten it right the first time. In business, every time you have to go back and redo something it costs the company money.

Commitment

Whenever I think about commitment, I think about the old joke; *whenever you see some bacon and eggs, remember the chicken was involved, but the pig was committed.*

There is a quote I like from the Optimist Creed about commitment...

OPTIMIST CREED

Promise Yourself

-To be so strong that nothing can disturb your peace of mind. To talk health, happiness and prosperity to every person you meet. To make all your friends feel that there is something in them. To look at the sunny side of everything and make your optimism come true. To think only of the best, to work only for the best and to expect only the best. To be just as enthusiastic about the success of others as you are about your own. To forget the mistakes of the past and press on to the greater achievements of

the future. To wear a cheerful countenance at all times and give every living creature you meet a smile. To give so much time to the improvement of yourself that you have no time to criticize others. To be too large for worry, too noble for anger, too strong for fear, and too happy to permit the presence of trouble.

-Optimist International

Teamwork

There's no "I" in team. People need to focus on developing strength in unity, on working together to understand how to achieve common goals. Leaders need to inspire and educate so their team stays enthusiastic and on task. Each individual needs to understand the purpose of their role and what their contribution is. It is up to the leader to send that message and to build the confidence and abilities of the team.

Responsibility

Enthusiasm

Sense of Purpose

Positive Attitude

Excellence

Commitment

Teamwork

The bottom line is we simply can't accomplish anything moving forward in business, in the world, unless we respect each other.

NOTES:

NOTES:

Notes:

CHAPTER THREE:
COMMUNITY

"Those who are lifting the world upward and onward, are those who encourage more than criticize"

–ELIZABETH HARRISON

"Whatever you do for yourself in life you take to your grave, but what you do for others, you leave behind with them."

~ LES BROWN

I BECAME INVOLVED IN COMMUNITY SERVICE a few years ago through Comcast. I had several motives for wanting to volunteer my time. My personal reasons, the ones that come from my heart, are my deepest reasons. I want to help inspire all children to realize that they can live their dreams. I want disadvantaged, inner-city kids, kids in gangs, to see me and hear my story in the hope that I can be a role model that they can relate. Like them, I came from a hard life, a poor childhood, and I made it into corporate America and a life of achievement, not failure. And I want Polynesian kids to see someone from their own culture who is successful. We have 150,00 Pacific Islanders in California now and we have virtually no one visible representing this population. The kids do not see adult Polynesian movie stars or newscasters, nor do they see their own faces in commercials. That's why I felt it was important for them to see me.

Another motive I have is best captured in the following quote form Les Brown.

"Happiness is like perfume. You can't put it on others without getting a few drops on yourself."

I believe that what I put into the world, I get back a thousand-fold. It helps my heart, it helps me be the person I want to be in this world, it keeps me in touch with what is important, and it opens doors and invites people into my life that I wouldn't have otherwise met.

I've had people ask me, Sai, how do I get this job that I want? I'm not really qualified, I don't have the credentials or know anybody in this company or field. I tell them one thing. Volunteer. Do it on your own time, on nights and weekends. Network: be visible. A lot of good workers go unseen. They are just too quiet. Nobody knows them.

Through the volunteer work I've done on behalf of my company, I am now on a first name basis with people in senior management that I wouldn't have known otherwise. I have been seen by 1.2 million people on TV, and I have gained more recognition in the community and at work. As people are getting to know my name, and me, it helps me personally and professionally. Most importantly it helps others, and keeps me in touch with my passion and message: Neither resistance to diversity, nor adversity, should stand in the way of creating a meaningful and successful life for yourself. If I can do it, anybody can.

Let me give you a few examples of the volunteer experiences I've had, to encourage you to get out there and do the same. These memories have enriched me and are now a part of who I am. I hope that I have touched a few lives along the way.

Where It All Began

COMCAST DOES AN ANNUAL, COMCAST CARES DAY, the first Saturday in October. In this event, we pick schools in the local area to help by doing such things as painting the school, doing yard work and building benches. Two years ago, I volunteered to be captain of a school project that was especially challenging. Nobody really wanted to mess with it. Our assignment was to clean out an eyesore junkyard in front of the school, dig out the weeds, cover it over with gravel, build benches and paint the entire wall near the cafeteria. Then we planted about twenty little flowerpots around the parameter of the schoolyard, beautifying it, and vastly improving the view.

It took almost ten hours of labor with 35 volunteers, men, women and children, working under my direction. It was a truly grueling day. However, we hit a home run. It was a victory for the company, the school system and the students. We not only satisfied the vision, Kathi Noe, our Director of Business Affairs, had for this project, but a month later, the principal of the school, and the San Mateo school system, voted Comcast the best company in the city for that year. I was asked by our Area Vice President to accept the award on

Comcast's behalf because he felt that my leadership and direction on this project had helped make it such a success. For me, the honor was in representing all the incredible volunteers who had put in so much effort to transform a school environment, from useless and ugly into a thing of beauty. At least in the eye of this beholder.

Motivating Children

"The way you get people to look up to you, is to not look down on them"

~ BRYAN "GATOR" WILSON

I VOLUNTEER TO DO MOTIVATIONAL SPEAKING IN schools. I do it because I want to inspire children, and because I want to give kids who are struggling a role model. I use my own life as a vehicle for talking about diversity and respect.

One of the schools I've volunteered to speak in is located in the projects of Sunnydale California, There is a large Samoan community there. That's what drew me. This was an opportunity for me to give back and to speak with children who, like me, came from the islands and whose lives were full of struggle, with many challenges to overcome. There were people who were pretty skeptical about how I could possibly have an influence with these students in one day. Did I really think I could reach these children? My reply was, you mean to tell me that if I only influence one child today, I haven't accomplished my job here?

I showed up wearing a suit and tie, professionally dressed. So what? Lots of adult men wear suits and ties. Except that I had brown skin and familiar features that they would recognize as being like them. I had one more thing going for me. Respect for where they were coming from. I was going to talk to them about the issue of diversity in our multicultural society because I knew they struggled with that in their own lives. I was going to use myself as an example and I was hoping that some of them might, if I was passionate enough, hear the message, respect yourself, and believe that they can be successful, no matter how impossible that seems in their own life, right here, right now. I wanted them to hear hope in my message and I wanted them to see me as an example of overcoming and winning the struggle.

I will possibly never know how many kids I've influenced by showing up and talking to them. Sometimes I get applause after I speak and sometimes it's hard to compete with teenage hormones in the older students who are busy checking each other out. I do know the younger students give me their full attention. There minds and ears are still open. But that doesn't mean I give up on the older ones. Because truly you never know when what you say or do takes root and starts to grow something inside someone. Mrs. Lee would probably be shocked to learn of the influence she had on me and how I have carried her words with me to this day.

I do have one example of a child I know I touched. Several months ago I participated in the *Principal For A Day* program, where I was assigned to the Kennedy Middle School in Redwood City, CA to speak to the students. I showed up with a camera crew. What child, no matter what their age, isn't going to be intrigued by that and think that this is something out of the ordinary, maybe even hope they might appear on camera themselves.

I went from class to class speaking to 7th and 8th graders. As I was leaving one class and on my way to another, a teacher caught up to me in the hall. She told me that the Pacific Islander students, especially one little Samoan girl, had been very captivated by me. There was a lot of buzz after I left the room. They were amazed that I was one of them. "You really made an impression on the kids who are from your culture," this teacher told me. "You are being a wonderful role model for them." That was very gratifying to hear and made my day.

Celebrating Diversity

OUR DIRECTOR OF MEDIA WAS LOOKING TO produce a thirty-second spot for TV called, "Comcast and the Community." Its purpose was to show what a diverse community works at Comcast. The director found out that I was from Hawaii, and he knew how quickly the Hawaiian population was growing in the Bay area, so he came to me and asked me for some ideas. I was excited because I thought this was a great opportunity to bring my culture into the mainstream, and what better way than through television?

I told him about my brother Michael's Hawaiian song and dance troupe, the "Academy of Hawaiian Arts in Oakland California." They had been selected by Universal Pictures during the making of Lilo and Stitch to model the choreography for the animation, to ensure that the Hawaiian dancing featured in the movie would be authentic. His troupe was chosen because they had the reputation for being the best Hawaiian dance group around.

I called my brother and we set up a date. We brought a camera crew to Oakland, CA one Tuesday night, and we shot a couple of dance scenes. Even I got into the action. I danced with my brother on TV! We had a blast. About 1.2 million people have seen the commercial on the local stations. I'd say that was pretty good exposure. I consider the campaign to have been a great success.

An Ongoing Commitment

COMMUNITY WORK IS AN ON-GOING COMMITMENT for me. I have a special mission to help other Polynesians adjust to, and thrive in American culture. I speak at local churches in the Samoan community. I am always seeking other projects and ways to contribute.

However, I have just as deep a commitment to my business community. I am passionate about motivating others to become great leaders and to lead great lives. In that spirit, I have embarked on a speaking tour of the Bay area on behalf of my company. I am grateful and excited by the opportunity to reach over 6,000 employees in the Bay area alone.

Throughout this book, I have used myself to exemplify behavior that I hope others will embrace. I believe that every person reading this book can find a place in their lives where they could improve. I believe that everyone is secretly or openly passionate about at least one thing, if not several things in their lives. The people who say they don't know what their passion is, should seek it, and commit to discovering it.

I have quoted so many people in this book. I want to add one more quote: my own.

"I believe all of us have a purpose in life: to live and to dream, to build and fulfill, to fail and to learn. We cannot prosper alone, nor succeed by traveling in empty, isolated valleys. It is only through the empowerment of people, the engaging energy of ideas, and by harnessing the creativity within you, that you can foster and manifest yourself into a higher place. Once you do, and only then, will you find your true destiny in life. It will be as though you possess a magic wand, bestowing a force and grace through you and within you, lifting you to a higher consciousness, allowing you to deliberately and consciously pursue your own calling to Greatness."

~SAITIA FAAIFO

NOTES:

NOTES:

CHAPTER FOUR:
EXERCISES

"I learned this at least, by my experiment: That if one advances confidently in the directions of his dreams, and endeavors to live the life which he has imagined, he will meet with a success unexpected in common hours. He will put some things behind, will pass an invisible boundary: New, universal, and more liberal laws will begin to establish around and within him, or the old law be expanded, and interpreted in his favor in a more liberal sense, and he will live with a license of a higher order of beings..........If you have built castles in the air, your work need not be lost, that is where, they should be. Now put the foundation under them."

~ HENRY DAVID THOREAU

Stick Person

ON THE FOLLOWING PAGE YOU WILL FIND A drawing of a stick person. It could be a man or a woman. This stick figure represents the potential you. It shows all the categories a person should possess to be a strong and skilled leader.

In this exercise, the goal is to look at yourself in the "mirror" and ask yourself, and then answer the question: Where do I stand in these categories?

For instance under the category Experience, write on the left side of the page all the things that you have accomplished that have added to your storehouse of experience and contributed to making you a good leader. Remember, it doesn't matter if you are a leader or not. And this doesn't have to be about a job. You can apply this to your family, your community, or to becoming the person you want to be.

On the right side of the paper list all the things that you need to improve or acquire in order to make your own Stick Person category complete.

Remember, you are the only person that is going to see this, so you need to be really honest with yourself if this exercise is going to be meaningful to you.

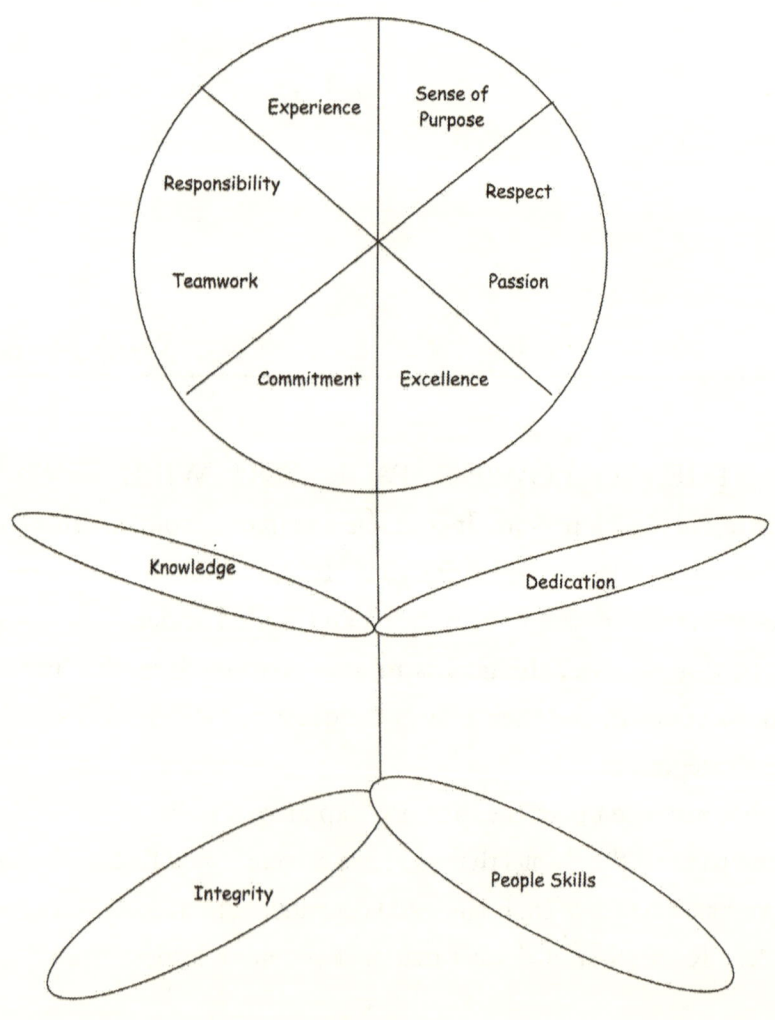

Qualities and Skills I need to Become The Leader I Want To Be

(Use a separate sheet of paper if you need it).

What Qualities/Skills Do I Possess?	What Qualities/Skills Do I Need?
<u>Examples:</u>	<u>Examples:</u>

1. Integrity   1. Integrity

2. People Skills   2. People Skills

3. Knowledge   3. Knowledge

4. Dedication

4. Dedication

5. Commitment

5. Commitment

6. Teamwork

6. Teamwork

7. Responsibility

7. Responsibility

8. Experience

8. Experience

9. Sense of Purpose

9. Sense of Purpose

10. Respect

10. Respect

11. Passion

11. Passion

12. Excellence

12. Excellence

Goal Setting

FIRST, I WANT YOU TO WRITE DOWN YOUR TOP TEN goals for the year. They should NOT be vague such as I want to become a better person. They need to be measurable, attainable and specific. Some of them also need to be slightly outside of your comfort zone, which make you ask yourself, "Can I *really* do this?"

I am showing you my list from two years ago as an example.

In January 2003, I wrote down my top ten goals to be completed by the end of the year. Almost all of them came true. I achieved 80 to 90% of them—and the ones that I didn't achieve, I rolled over into the next year and reset my goals. It is a very powerful experience to see what happens when you write your goals down on paper, and read them once a day or several times a day, every week.

Also, visualize your goals. If you want a promotion, picture yourself shaking hands with your boss and thanking him or her. How does it make you feel? What's the dialogue? Think of what you, he or she might say.

Maybe you want a new car. Cut out a picture of that car. Be specific. What make and model? What color? What features? Imagine yourself in it driving. Is the wind in your hair? Have you got the music cranked up?

Here is the list of my goals from 2003.

1. Receive another promotion with my company
2. Be the greatest motivational speaker I can be
3. Improve my financial status
4. Become a better listener
5. Improve my leadership skills-become a better manager
6. Start to write my book
7. Be a better father
8. Inspire thousands into achieving their dreams and greatness
9. Save money
10. Buy my mom a car.

Now set your top ten goals:

1.

2.

3.

4.

5.

6.

7.

8.

9.

10.

Next I want you to write down your top three goals that you want to accomplish in the next month. Again, they should NOT be vague. They should be measurable, attainable and specific. Something like I want to read a book a week for the next month. Or, I will enroll in that computer tech class that I have been putting off, and get my certification. They should also be building blocks toward achieving your year-end goals.

Write them here and then copy them on an index card. You should carry this index card around with you and look at it several times a day. You can even make a second copy and put it up on your mirror or refrigerator, or your car dashboard.

Even though you may feel foolish, say them out loud.

Every month reset your goals. Every day look at your monthly goals. Every week look at your yearly goals. As you meet you monthly goals move them off your list and set new ones. Remember you are moving yourself toward your bigger, annual goals.

Here's the great news. If you don't make a particular monthly goal, forgive yourself, tell yourself you are in the process of achieving these goals, and once achieved, you will be in the process of achieving the next set. Looking back you will discover all the progress you have made and realize you have in fact exceeded your original goals!

Write your three goals here.

1.

2.

3.

Today or tomorrow, copy them onto an index card.

I truly believe that the "universal laws" will open up for you as you move towards your goals.

In Conclusion

Thank you for spending the time you have taken to complete this book. I would like to leave you with the words of a traditional Hawaiian song that stirs memories in me and is sung when parting. To me the song is very lovely and expresses how I feel in ending this journey with you.

Aloha,
Saitia Faaifo

ALOHA 'OE

Ha'aheo ka ua i na pali,	Proudly sweeps the rain clouded by the cliffs,
Ke nihi a`e la i ka nahele,	As onward it glides through the trees,
E uhai ana paha i ka liko,	It seems to be following the liko,
Pua ahihi lehua a o uka.	The ahihi lehua of the vale.
(Chorus)	(Chorus)
Aloha `oe, aloha `oe,	Farewell to thee, farewell to thee,
E ke onaona noho i ka lipo,	Thou charming one who dwells among
One fond embrace a ho`i a`e au,	the bowers.
Until we meet again.	One fond embrace before I now depart
	Until we meet again.

If I had my life to live over, I'd try
To make more mistakes next time. I would
Relax, I would limber up, I would be crazier
Than I've been on this trip. I know very
Few things I'd take seriously any more.
I would take more chances, I would take more
Trips, I would scale more mountains,
I would swim more rivers, and I would
Watch more sunsets. I would eat more
Ice cream and fewer beans.
I would have more actual troubles
And fewer imaginary ones. You see...
I was one of those people who lived
Prophylactically and sensibly and sanely,
Hour after hour and day after day.
Oh, I've had my moments
And, if I had to do it all over
Again, I'd have many more of them.
In fact, I'd try not to have anything
Else, just moments, one after another
Instead of living so many
Years ahead of my day. I've been
One of those people who never went anywhere without
A thermometer, a hot water bottle, a gargle, a
Raincoat and a parachute.
If I had it to do all over again,
I'd travel lighter, much lighter,
Than I have.
I would start barefoot earlier
In the spring, and I'd stay that way
Later in the fall. And I would

Ride more merry-go-rounds, and
Catch more gold rings, and greet
More people, and pick more flowers,
And dance more often. If I had it
To do all over again.
But you see,
I don't.

- AN 82 YEAR OLD DYING MAN
FROM JOURNAL OF HUMANISTIC PSYCHOLOGY

"If you don't plant flowers in your mind, than weeds will grow by default"

B<small>RAIN</small> T<small>RACY</small>

If you want a thing bad enough to go out and fight for it, to work day and night for it, to give up your time, your peace, and your sleep for it...if all that you dream and scheme is about it, and life seems useless and worthless without it...if you gladly sweat for it and fret for it and plan for it and lose all your terror of the opposition for it...if you simply go after that thing you want with all of your capacity, strength and sagacity, faith, hope and confidence and stern pertinacity...if neither cold, poverty, famine, nor gout, sickness nor pain, of body and brain, can keep you away from the thing that you want... if dogged and grim you beseech and beset it, with the help of God, you WILL get it! —

LES BROWN, LIVE YOUR DREAMS

"The more you learn, the more you earn, than you can give back in return"

LES BROWN.

Today upon a bus I saw a girl with golden hair;
she seemed so gay, I envied her, and wished that I were half so fair;
watched her as she rose to leave, and saw her hobble down the aisle.
She had one leg and wore a crutch, but as she passed – a smile.
Oh, God, forgive me when I whine;
I have two legs – the world is mine.
Later on I bought some sweets. The boy who sold them had such charm,
I thought I'd stop and talk awhile. If I were late, t'would do no harm.
And as we talked he said, "Thank you, sir, you've really been so kind.
It's nice to talk to folks like you because, you see, I'm blind."
Oh, God, forgive me when I whine;
I have two eyes – the world is mine.
Later, walking down the street, I met a boy with eyes so blue.
But he stood and watched the others play, it seemed he knew not
*   what to do.*
I paused, and then I said, "Why don't you join the others, dear?"
But he looked straight ahead without a word, and then I knew, he
*   couldn't hear.*
Oh, God forgive me when I whine;
I have two ears – the world is mine.
Two legs to take me where I go,
two eyes to see the sunset's glow,
two ears to hear all I should know,
oh, God, forgive me when I whine;
I'm blessed, indeed, the world is mine.

- DR. TENNYSON GUYER

NOTES:

NOTES:

NOTES:

NOTES:

NOTES: